Sakagwa's Ghost

Enock Bitugi Matundura

Translated by Kefa Otiso

Nsemia

First Edition (translation): November 2020
Published by Nsemia Inc. Publishers (www.nsemia. com); Oakville, Otario, Canada

Edited By: Sally Boyani Mokaya
Cover Concept: Author
Cover Design: Robert Kambo Maina
Layout: Bethsheba Nyabuto
Production Consultant: Matunda Nyanchama

Note for Librarians:
A cataloguing record for this book is available from the Library and Archives Canada

ISBN: 978-1-926906-76-8

Dedication

I dedicate this book to the memory of my late grandfather, Onsando Agutta, my late grandmother, Birisira Kerubo, and my late paternal uncle, John Mamboleo Onsando.

Acknowledgements

The publication of this book is a collective effort of various individuals. It has been a fifteen-year journey and I must say it was worth the wait. To the team, thank you. Allow me to prioritise my gratitude in equal measure; on the premise that a lot of individuals and various factions have contributed towards achieving the final copy.

I will first credit my publisher, Nsemia Inc. In brutal honesty, it was not easy to get a publisher to adopt the manuscript of *Sakagwa's Ghost*. Perhaps, it is a subject that most publishers cower from.

As it turns out, Dr. Matunda Nyanchama had noted the existing literary gap on the legendary Gusii hero Sakagwa Ng'iti. This gap has existed for a long time. Either the stories of African legends have always been ignored or there has been lack of boldness on the part of authors and publishers to bring them out. There could be other reasons that have led to stories of African legends being overlooked. They include the lack of writers willing to conduct primary research and write works (creative or otherwise) on our African legends for the benefit of future generations.

Consequently, Dr. Nyanchama advertised for book proposals of this genre. I responded and he devotedly embraced the idea behind the book. That is how the publication of *Sakagwa's Ghost* came to pass.

I thank Professor Angaluki Muaka who worked hard to polish an earlier draft of this book. I recognise your astute commitment.

Secondly, I profoundly appreciate the contributions of the various elders of Bogeka village in Kisii County. This is where legend Sakagwa Ng'iti is believed to have been born, raised, and lived. In particular, I single out elder Maisiba Gisemba. He gave me the benefit of folktales on Sakagwa, stories that were common knowledge in their generation. Unfortunately, this ancient wisdom has been distorted and diluted through chronology of time.

This book has bridged a wide literary void of losing or altering Sakagwa's legend, which has always been orally passed from one generation to the next.

Thirdly, I am grateful to Prof. William Robert Ochieng' (now deceased) of Maseno University. He is well versed with the history of the Abagusii. As a matter of fact, it was the subject of his PhD dissertation. Whenever I needed clarity on various historical aspects of the Abagusii, I consulted him. It was an in-depth consultation especially since I disagreed with him on some aspects.

Fourthly, I recognize my paternal uncle, Mzee Orioba Onsando. He gave me the preparatory foundation that enabled me to research and collect data that helped me to narrate this tale. Moreover, I am equally grateful to Mr. Elkana Ong'esa. He relished the thought of a book like this and always encouraged me to keep writing it whenever I was on the verge of giving up.

Nevertheless, I wish to caution readers that even though Sakagwa truly lived, the Sakagwa who is the main character in this book is fictional and is therefore quite different from the historical Sakagwa. Consequently, if there is any contradiction between the real and fictional Sakagwa, historical accuracy should not be used to judge the validity of this work. Art or fiction and history are different subjects that should be scrutinised on their own merits. A work of art or fiction is never censured for its historicity but for the violation of the rules of art.

I save my cordial appreciation for my family. Dear brother, Dr. James Micah Onsando and your lovely wife, Mrs. Margaret Kemuma Onsando; I thank you for raising and nurturing me to thrive in the academic world. You played an integral role in moulding the man that I am today.

I am eternally indebted to my parents, Mzee Micah Matundura Onsando and my mothers[1], Rebecca Mokeira and Miriam Nyangweso. We are grateful for your valuable contribution in raising, educating, and serving as role models to us in this uncertain changing world of today.

I give a notable tribute to the reviewers of the foundational drafts of this book. Their valuable recommendations helped refine the raw manuscript. The reviewers include my teachers, Hezron Mogambi, Dr. Kyallo Wadi Wamitila, Kineene wa Mutiso of the University of Nairobi and my friend, Mr. Samuel Ng'ang'a Irungu. In addition, I thank Dr. Mwenda Mukuthuria, Director of the Board of Postgraduate Studies of Chuka University, for agreeing to proofread the book despite his heavy administrative responsibilities.

Without forgetting, I thank my teacher and friend Prof. Nathan Oyori Ogechi, the Deputy Vice-Chancellor,

---

[1] In polygamous families in Gusii, children traditionally refer to their mothers' co-wives or step-mothers as mothers.

Moi University, for agreeing to write the preface of this book in spite of his demanding schedule.

I save my last appreciations to my loving wife and friend, Lilian Mokeira Arama, my son, Ernest Griffin Matundura (Jnr) and my nephew, Clinton Matundura for their patience and support while I was scripting this literature. To all: *mbuya mono* (i.e., thank you in Ekegusii).

Bitugi Matundura,
June 23, 2010
Chuka University College

Foreword to the English Translation

It is my privilege to present to you the English translation of Bitugi Matundura's Kiswahili book, *Kivuli cha Sakawa* [*Sakagwa's Ghost*[1]]. When I first read it, I was struck by the significance of the work given the scarcity of published works in Gusii oral literature. Works of this stature are urgently needed to document the rapidly eroding traditional cultures such as those of Abagusii. The erosion of this culture is due to the avalanche of European cultural influences and the gradual depletion of the elderly population that either witnessed or heard it firsthand from those who lived the experiences. Moreover, rapid urbanization and cultural change in Gusii is increasingly undermining the vitality of the Ekegusii language. While this work will not stem the tide against the Ekegusii language and culture, it will at least help to preserve its speakers' knowledge base for posterity.

Works such as *Sakagwa's Ghost* not only help preserve but also spread traditional Gusii knowledge within and outside of the rapidly globalizing Gusii community. It also adds to the global cultural milieu, enriching it in the process.

To an extent, this English translation of *Kivuli cha Sakawa*, will contribute to the preservation and possible recovery of some relevant aspects of Kenya's, and indeed Africa's indigenous knowledge, culture, and history. As we know, much of the written record

[1] Please note that in this translation we have adopted the name Sakagwa (as it would be spelt in Kisii) rather than Sakawa as used by the author in the Kiswahili version

of Africa's oral literature has until recently been done by outsiders: missionaries, travelers, scholars or colonialists. Consequently, such works have often been histories of various outsiders about Africa and not the histories of local people as they know them. As an African scholar, I am privileged to have had a chance to play a small role in the preservation and possible revival of relevant aspects of indigenous Gusii culture and knowledge.

Accordingly, I dedicate this translation to the vitality of future generations of the Abagusii community.

Kefa M Otiso, PhD
Professor of Geography
Bowling Green State University
Bowling Green, Ohio, USA
January 24, 2018

Preface

Kiswahili readers have, among other books, read *Sundiata*, *Kinjeketile*, and *Mukwava wa Uhehe*. Although *Sundiata*, *Kinjeketile*, and *Mukwava* are important historical figures in our African communities, books written on their significance are fictional rather than historical. These works serve a great role in immortalising these historical characters and their ethnic communities. Books of this genre remind us of legends from various communities and how they are perceived in their respective communities. However, until now, I have not been lucky to come across any book written on historical figures of the Abagusii community. Nevertheless, I have met many Abagusii community members who lament over the loss of their history and culture in part because there are no books on these subjects. In that context, Matundura's book, *Sakagwa's Ghost* is an important step towards preserving the name and memory of Sakagwa, the legendary leader of the Abagusii people. Besides preserving Sakagwa's name, this book also contributes to the preservation of the oral literature of the Abagusii.

The author, Enock Bitugi Matundura, is an emerging expert in Kiswahili, specialising in fictional and creative writing in the distinguished language of Kiswahili. The story that he narrates herein demonstrates his high sense of creativity; he uses his community's folktales to recreate a symbolic work of art. Matundura's hard work speaks for itself. In less than ten years, he has written a number of books.

His writings have been published by various firms in Kenya. His other published works include: a collection of short stories, notably, his 2008 book, *Sitaki Iwe Siri [I don't want it to be a secret]*. It took second place in the Jomo Kenyatta Prize for Literature in 2009. Undoubtedly, this is an author of highly cherished works.

Matundura has demonstrated language competence in this tale of Sakagwa. The book is rich with figures of speech. He uses proverbs and similes in an exclusive manner. Matundura does justice to this piece of fiction by narrating it in a captivating style that compels the reader from the start to the end of the story. The writer frequently uses Ekegusii words to convey crucial Gusii[1] cultural concepts with an intention to preserve the culture of the Abagusii people. He provides accurate translations, which enable the reader to follow the story easily. The approach used is well calculated not to divert the attention of a non Gusii reader. This is a unique talent. Besides suitable illustrations, there is a glossary at the end of the book that a reader can refer to understand Ekegusii words used in the volume.

The book comprises of thirteen thought-provoking short chapters, which take us through Sakagwa's audacious life.

In the opening chapter, the author paints to us a vivid picture of Sakagwa's father, Mzee Ng'iti, and his family of two wives. He shows us the tribulations that befell Ng'iti in his desperate search for a son and heir[2] to the point of sacrificing to God and his Abagusii ancestors.

---

[1] The term Gusii can stand for the Abagusii people or their habitat.
[2] As the Gusii are a patriarchal society, only sons are considered to be worthy heirs.

Consequently, when Sakagwa is born, we are shown how elder Ng'iti celebrates and teaches his son the history and culture of his community, and the skills of a herbalist. Later, we encounter the unfortunate death of Elder Ng'iti, which welcomes Sakagwa's succession as the new leader of his community. By design, the heir takes over all the leadership responsibilities. The story unfolds the sequential conflicts that he encountered earlier to how he grew to be an exemplary leader. He helped his community win wars against neighboring ethnic communities. The author narrates the prophecies that Sakagwa gave the community. The apex of these prophecies was the coming of European colonialists who were to alienate his community's land, which came to pass after his death. Without a doubt, this is an essential work from an insightful author. I therefore recommend it to be read by all who value culture and oral literature.

Nathan Oyori Ogechi
Eldoret, June 2010

Nathan Oyori Ogechi is the Deputy Vice-Chancellor, Students Affair at Moi University, Eldoret, Kenya.

Table of Contents

Dedication iii

Acknowledgements v

Foreword to the English Translation ix

Preface.. xi

1. The Wish 1

2. The Sacrifice 9

3. A New Song 17

4. Divinatory Training 23

5. The Origin and Culture of Abagusii 27

6. Mzee Ng'iti's Death... 35

7. The Puzzle Solved 41

8. The Great Calamity 47

9. Unity is Strength 53

10. The Battle of Saosao 59

11. The Farewell Party 65

12. The "Death" of Sakagwa 71

13. Sakagwa's Ghost 77

14. Glossary of Terms 86

About the Author 89

1. The Wish

It was at the break of dusk and the sun was setting splendidly into the horizon,   showering the hills with its amber fiery-like rays. It bade and kissed them goodbye. As if on cue, the hills cheered in joy and glee responding to the sun's last adieu.

Birds danced with happiness in the sky while others perched on trees, sending off the sun with a silent cheer. As usual, their intention was to clock off into their nests as soon as the sun went past the horizon.

At Elder Ng'iti's homestead, dusk was fast creeping in; the livestock hastened their last activities of the day before going off to rest for the night. The cows returning from their pastures were heard mooing, craving for their calves' presence, "moo moo" for they had gone daylong without seeing their young ones. With pointed tails, the calves responded with great vitality, playfully jumping up and down. To the young cows, it was only a matter of moments before they suckled to their preferred satisfaction.

In contrast, cows without calves remained calm as a summer sea. Unbothered with happenings in their surroundings, they chewed the cud that they had hoarded from daylong grazing. As the saying goes, loneliness is not a fault but a condition of existence.

Hens and their chicks scratched hurriedly in the grass for any spilled grains to satiate their hunger pangs and those of their chicks.

Simba[1], a huge, fierce black dog in Elder Ng'iti's homestead was curled-up and fast asleep on a heap

of millet chaff that had been dumped at the gate to the homestead. He was calmly resting, probably waiting for the night, with much anticipation and pensiveness, so as to undertake his duty of guarding the homestead.

On the other hand, both of elder Ng'iti's wives were not slacking behind either. They were as busy as bees determined to complete their tasks in preparation for the night. Mzee Ng'iti's first wife, Bochere, was almost done with gathering the finger millet that she had been sun drying. She was struggling to fold the large cow

---

[1] Means lion in Kiswahili and is a popular name for fierce guard dogs in Gusii.

hide that she used to dry the millet before returning it to the house to await use the next day. After this, she was expected to go to the cattle shed with her lastborn daughter, Nyakerario, to milk the cows. Her older daughters, who had helped her with this task for several years, were now married.

Meanwhile, the second wife, Bochaberi, was using two special stones: hand grain mill, *ensio** and *orogena** to grind millet into flour that would be used for preparing *ugali* for supper. Her four daughters were helping her. They scooped the grain with their palms and poured it on the large millstone, *orogena*, where it was ground to flour.

As the girls poured the grain on the *orogena*, their mother promptly and methodically used *ensio* to grind it into flour. Today it is rare to find implements such as *ensio** and *orogena* (hand grain mills) being used[2]* due to the widespread use of modern electric motor and diesel engine flour mills. Nevertheless, in those days, the *ensio* and *orogena* hand grain milling technology was dominant.

Bochere was approximately fifty years old. She was short with a dark complexion. Her hardworking nature compared to no other. Every year she harvested a satisfactory amount of millet, enough to fill several storehouses. Her hard work satiated Mzee Ng'iti's family food needs year in year out. As a result, the term "hunger" was foreign to this family. To add to her many attributes, Bochere was always cheerful, except when she remembered the dispute she had

---

[2] Indian traders (and their graves) are very rare in modern Gusii because of their tiny populations and their being forced out of local retail trades by natives. Indians dominated this business in colonial Kenya.

with her husband for many years. She, however, hated revisiting that agonizing memory lane because it concerned life and could easily end her marriage. Nevertheless, the Swahili sages were not wrong when they declared that *wagombanao ndio wapatanao,* those who quarrel are also the ones who reconcile; no dispute is permanent.

Their marriage of many years was threatened. It could fall apart because Bochere had failed to bear Mzee Ng'iti a son. Their firstborn child Kerubo, a girl, was followed by more girls, including Moraa, Nyaboke, twins Barongo and Nyaituga, and the last born Nyanchera. All these girls were now married and Bochere's house was practically an "empty nest".

Although Mzee Ng'iti subscribed to his Abagusii community's proverb that, *'nyomba ya baiseke bange 'nkerandi getakuoma**, a family with many girls is like a gourd that never runs out of milk (it is constantly replenished by dowry payments - cows). Not having a heir was his greatest worry! The son would inherit his vast wealth and carry on with their family's lineage. Failure to have a son, in his view and that of the community, was not only shameful but also dangerous.

"Girls, girls …girls … what kind of a wife are you, who can't bear me a son?" Bochere kept recalling how the dispute between her and her husband had started. What once appeared like a slight disagreement had escalated to an endless dispute.

"Aren't daughters as good as sons?" Bochere kept asking, not knowing that such questions annoyed her husband. They pricked his heart like hot nails on a wound. He could beat Bochere on a daily basis while threatening her with divorce and marrying a second wife.

She became Mzee Ng'iti's punching bag until Bochere could not bear it anymore! She one day lost her temper and shouted at him, "Children are children, whether female or male, both are blessings from our ancestors! Sons and daughters are all equal! Moreover, conception is not one person's work. It involves a husband and a wife."

"What insolence! How rude of you! A wife fails to bear me a son and then insults me? I will teach her manners by marrying a second wife. She will then know that I am the head of this family." Ng'iti replied angrily.

That is how Bochaberi joined the family. Mzee Ng'iti's second wife was a slim, dark-skinned woman of few words.

After one year of marriage, Bochaberi bore Ng'iti a daughter. "Never mind! The second one will be a son," Mzee Ng'iti comforted himself.

However, things did not go as he had wished. Bochaberi continued bearing one daughter after another. When the fourth daughter was born, Mzee Ng'iti became exceedingly worried.

He still did not have the solution to the inheritance dilemma! There was no one to inherit his vast wealth, coming mainly from his renowned skills of a witch doctor; wealth that was growing day and night. Every time he brought up this issue with his second wife, she empathized with his situation. It saddened her that she had been unable to bear him a son. Her life in marriage with Mzee Ng'iti had followed a path similar to that of her co-wife, Bochere. In Mzee Ngiti's time, only sons could inherit their father's wealth. Women could only get indirect benefits through their husbands. This is in contrast to modern times where both daughters and sons have equal entitlement to their parents' wealth.

Without a male child Mzee Ngiti was a worried man especially with old age catching up. Although this saddened him deeply, he did not lose hope. He strongly believed that his younger wife would still bear him a heir.

One evening, Mzee Ng'iti was on his way home from the forest where he had gone to look for his medicinal herbs that he used to treat patients. It was his routine every day to go to the forest starting early in the morning. He would collect an assortment of herbs which he could use the herbs to treat people from all over Gusii and also the neighbouring communities of the Maasai, Luo and Kipsigis. This occupation made him a highly respected elder within these communities. That is why each day that passed without him having a son deeply troubled him and gave him no peace of mind. He had to bear a son to inherit his wealth and the community role or else his lineage and skill would be forgotten in a few generations. He needed divine intervention! As a last resort, he resolved to make a sacrifice to God, *Engoro*[3], and his ancestors.

When supper was ready, Mzee Ng'iti was served in different bowls from those of his family members as was teh norm. It was customary in the Abagusii community for the head of household to eat with his sons while his wives ate with their daughters. It was prohibited for anyone to eat before the head of the family prayed to the ancestors. Thus, at every mealtime especially during supper, Mzee Ng'iti led these prayers.

Elder Ng'iti chomped two morsels of the millet *ugali* from his *ekee*[4] (bowl), a small piece followed by a big piece as he stood from his favourite three-legged round stool. He made three steps to the door of his hut. He then turned around. With his back to the door, he threw the big piece of *ugali* over his shoulder saying, "...there's your gift our creator, *Engoro*, who gives this family good health and life as well as male and female children."

Shortly afterwards, he also threw the small piece of *ugali* and said, "...and there is the gift to our ancestors Mogusii, Osogo, Moluguhia, Kigoma, Ribiaka and

---

[3] The God of Abagusii.
[4] A large traditional serving bowl weaved using dry millet straw and tied with animal hide at the bottom.

Kintu..." He then walked back to his seat, looked at it for a while before sitting down. On sitting down, the whole family started to eat heartily in silence. Elder Ng'iti ate his food in his own company, lost in deep thoughts.

"If only I had a son to join me in eating this food," he mused at heart. "Never mind! The mercies of our ancestors will help me to get a heir."

Not far from him, his wives and daughters enjoyed their meal. With relish, they ate the millet *ugali* with bitter vegetables *chinsaga* (African Spider Flower or *Cleome gynandra*) as they talked in low tones.

Once they had eaten to their fill, Mzee Ng'iti told his wives that, in a few days' time, they would go together to Manga Escarpment to offer a big sacrifice and pray to *Engoro*[5].

---

[5] Abagusii have traditionally considered the rocks and cave of the scenic Manga escarpment near Kisii town to be sacred shrines of *Engoro*(God) and their ancestors. They have thus used the site to beseech *Engoro* and their ancestors for solutions to various natural and social problems such as droughts, barrenness, and illnesses.

2. The Sacrifice

Eventually, all preparations for the sacrifice at Manga escarpment were completed. The preparations made were beyond comparison to any that had happened before. Mzee Ng'iti and his two wives, Bochere and Bochaberi, made sure that all the essentials required for the sacrifice were ready. There was no room for error!

Among the things they readied were: a big bundle of firewood tied with dry banana stalk twine, a huge he-goat with a long beard like that of an Indian Sikh, a white cock, two bowls of millet flour, a bunch of bananas, a sharp knife, an oil lamp, a fly whisk, and two gouds of sour milk.

Mzee Ng'iti had sent word to Mzee Kebabe Okioma about the planned journey. He wanted the help of Okioma's son, Maikara. He was a strong young man aged about twenty three years, who would help with carrying the he-goat to the site of the sacrifice site at Manga Escarpment.

In his days of youth, Ng'iti would not need such help as he had the strength. Now that he was old and weak, he needed help. He sought this from his fellow elder, Kebabe Okioma, who had sons. This act brought immeasurable pain to his heart; it opened a sore wound and a constant reminder of his sorry state of lack of a heir. However, he was hopeful that after the sacrifice, his situation will change for the better.

The day of the sacrifice finally came. By the time of the first cockcrow, Mzee Ng'iti, his wives, and Maikara Okioma were on their way to the caves at Manga Escarpment. Ng'iti led the way with his bag of medicines hanging from the 7-shaped walking stick on his left shoulder. He used the spear in his right hand for balance as he walked measurably through the rough terrain.

Behind him came Maikara who was carrying the he-goat on his shoulders and holding its legs firmly over his chest. Maikara was followed by Bochere balancing a large bundle of firewood on her head. Her co-wife, Bochaberi, also trudged along balancing a bulky basket on her head. Among things inside the basket was the sacrificial cock with its head peeking, facing where they had come from.

Simba leisurely trailed behind them as if uncertain whether he was allowed to be part of the journey. He had made up his mind that, come what may, he was not going to be left behind. Mzee Ng'iti's attempts to get him to stay home had failed. Simba had on numerous occasions accompanied his master to the forest. Perhaps, this defiance of his master's order to stay behind came from their regular trips to the forest that had now become a routine. Simba appeared to believe that it was his right to be part of the big trip that the family was undertaking.

It was a new spectacle for Simba to see a cock and a he-goat being carried. As a clever dog, he connected the dots and knew that there will be food whatever the journey's destination turned out to be, concluding that a good meal would be part of this trip. Simba was definitely not a stupid dog when Ng'iti chased him away several times, he could run into one bush and come out through another. He did this repeatedly until Mzee Ng'iti gave up and let him participate in that special trip.

Simba was a stubborn dog. Occasionally, when he made up his mind to do something, he could not

listen to anybody come what may. He seemed to have decided to participate in the trip and his stubbornness helped him to achieve his objective, just like it is said, *ukitaka cha mvungni shart uinamae*[6] (whoever requires something has to work hard to get it). Simba relied on his stubbornness and managed to get what he wanted. Otherwise, Simba would have remained hungry.

Soon, Simba led the way. He went from bush to bush with his tongue out displaying his mouth wide open. His tail was curled into an "O", defending its purpose of covering his behind. At times, he unfolded his tail and wagged it from side to side in happiness.

After travelling for about one and half hours, the sun started rising from the east. Whispers of wind could <u>be heard, and</u> with a light feathery touch, they cleared

[6] This is a popular Swahili proverb.

the fog as they swayed trees. Schools of clouds silently swept across the sky without any signs of a downpour.

Mzee Ng'iti led his family through leaf-covered shortcuts in the forest. He was well-versed with footpaths in the forest due to many years of excursions in search of herbal medicine in the forest. His wives and Maikara followed him closely, like cattle going to the slaughter-house.

Soon, the sky stabbing peak of Manga Ridge appeared in the distant horizon. After a trek of what seemed like two and a half hours, they arrived at the caves of Manga Ridge. It was about seven-thirty in the morning. Each of Mzee Ng'iti's wives placed her luggage down to catch a breath and, at least, rest for a while. They were gasping for air and sweating profusely due to the long, non-stop journey. On the other hand, Mzee Ng'iti and Maikara appeared not to have broken a sweat!

Without wasting time, Elder Ng'iti and Maikara untied the bundle of firewood. Then they took the banana leaves and a sharp knife. Behind a nearby bush, they spread the banana leaves on the ground, and slaughtered the he-goat on them. They drained the dead animal's blood into the *ekee** they had brought along. They skinned the goat and cut the carcass into big chunks of meat. Simba sat close by watching, licking his mouth and salivating like a greedy hyena.

When Mzee Ng'iti was done with the task of preparing the meat, he started lighting a fire. The task turned out stressful because of the headstrong wind which put out the fire every time he tried. With unrelenting efforts of sheltering the fire from the wind, Ngi'ti finally managed to get a stead flame burning. Simba remained where the goat had been slaughtered, nosing and licking blood spilt on the banana leaves.

Mzee Ng'iti then started cooking the meat that had been cut into pieces. When they were well cooked, he took the cooked pieces of meat and asked his wives to roast them. As the meat was roasting, Mzee Ng'iti took a brand of fire and went into the pitch dark cave carrying a bowl of blood from the goat along with a fly whisk. The smoking brand of fire, which left behind smoke clouds like a diesel train, barely provided enough light to see through the darkness as he had anticipated.

As he entered the cave, a colony of bats that had made the cave their dwelling, flew out at lightning speed. They made noise as they angrily protested against interruption of their morning rest. Undoubtedly, they had hunted all night long and needed to take a breather. Harsh screeches of bats echoed across the cave. However, Mzee Ng'iti was not in any way worried of the creatures. He knew that, just like croaking frogs cannot prevent cattle from drinking water from a river, neither can the shrieks of bats put a stop to what he had set to undertake in the caves. The bat's screeches were futile noises like those of a barking dog that cannot bite.

He got to the place of the cave that he wanted. Here, he sat down, dipped his fly whisk into the bowl of blood and sprinkled it to every corner of the cave as he uttered these words:

Engoro, you who gave health to the descendants of Kintu,
Engoro, you who gave our forefathers children,
Children of both sexes,
Daughters to procreate,

Sons to be heirs.
Daughters you have given me in abundance. Thanks!
Thank you for such blessings.
A son, I do not have! Even one! You have denied me.
Why?
Now I have no heir, yet am aging,
Engoro, Creator of the sun, the moon and the stars,
If there is anyone in my homestead who has offended
you,
Be it my wives or daughters,
Here is a blood sacrifice for you,
DRINK!

Mzee Ng'iti spent about half an hour reciting these words after which he emerged from the cave. At the entrance, he stood as still as an ebony tree, with his eyes fixed on the sun without blinking. It was a prayerful gaze. He had to do this for, in the sun, is where *Engoro* lived and he needed to connect with

this God of Abagusii and their ancestors. He looked miserable as tears trickled down his cheeks forming two paths on either side of his face like a procession of camels.

Once he finished, he went straight to where his wives were. He instructed them to get the meat that had been cooking, sour milk in containers, the oil lamp, and follow him to the cave. Mzee Ng'iti led the way with his wives in tow. As they got close to the cave, the women hesitated to go past the entrance. They were scared by the agonizing darkness in the cave.

Meanwhile, Maikara remained outside with his arms folded across his chest. He was taken aback and openly puzzled by what Mzee Ng'iti was doing. In his life, he had never seen a sacrifice being offered. On that day, he was as lucky as a child born on Friday,[7] to have witnessed a traditional Abagusii sacrifice. A few moments later, he went to watch over some of the meat that was still roasting especially since Simba was showing menacing signs of stealing the meat.

"Light the oil lamp quickly," Mzee Ng'iti directed his wives when he realized that they were afraid to follow him into the cave. "It is pitch dark in here," he added.

The two women appeared to fumble as they jointly worked to light the lamp.

"Hey!" Mzee Ng'iti exclaimed. "Make haste, women! We have no more time to waste," he hastened to add as he blew his stuffed nose and wiped drying tears from his eyes with the palms of his hands.

A while later, they got inside the cave. Mzee Ng'iti told them to kneel down with their backs to the entrance

---

[7] Muslims consider any child born on their holy day of Friday to be highly blessed by God, Allah.

of the cave. He then took the meat they were carrying and threw pieces of it to various corners of the cave. While doing so, he uttered unintelligible words while circling his wives. He did this for what looked like an eternity for the two women who knelt patiently lest they face *Engoro's* wrath.

When he finished, he took some of the remaining pieces of meat and put a piece each in his wives' mouths, directing them to chew and swallow the meat. They did so. Finally, he asked them to stand up and walk backwards out of the cave with their eyes closed. They obeyed.

Once outside, Mzee Ng'iti took two bowls of millet flour and spread it on their faces while uttering the same unintelligible words he had uttered in the cave. Next, he poured the remaining flour near the entrance to the cave. He then took his spear and thrust it into the ground near the entrance to cave.

Outside, Maikara, as if under Simba's watch, remained busy roasting the rest of the meat while waiting for Mzee Ng'iti to finish offering his sacrifice.

Mzee Ng'iti finally concluded his sacrifice. He then ordered his wives to pack the rest of the meat in a basket in readiness for their journey back home. Ng'iti asked his second wife to go throw the white cock into the cave. Once she had done so, they promptly left the place without looking back.

Although the journey home had begun, Simba remained behind looking for chunks of meat in the cave while chewing bones with his tough teeth.

3. A New Song

Towards the end of the second year after Mzee Ng'iti's big sacrifice at Manga Ridge, his second wife Bochaberi became conceived. Mzee Ng'iti had high hopes that this time around a male heir would be born in his homestead. He did not pay attention to the warning against counting one's chicks before they hatch. Mzee Ng'iti began to make preparations to receive the son that he had been waiting for over many years.

God does not abandon his servant, Ng'iti believed. Thus, days turned to weeks and weeks became months. As days in the ninth month of Bochaberi's pregnancy passed, a new song was about to be sang in Mzee Ng'iti's homestead. It would be welcome relief for a man of advanced age. He was getting "as old as the hills", in the minds of many in the community.

One day, under the pinkish wash of a setting sun, Bochaberi started to experience labour pains. Agony was written all over her face as if crabs were clinging on her intestines and slowly tightening their grip. In alarm, her co-wife, Bochere, hurriedly went to seek assistance from Saringi, a renown midwife in the Bogeka clan.

Saringi had a stout frame of unapologetic thick thighs, and a foreshowing large behind that made her walk like a duck. When she was informed that there was work for her in Mzee Ng'iti's homestead, she took her midwifery paraphernalia and accompanied Bochere to beat the drum that she had played for many years. Saringi was highly respected in the community for her role of ushering in new life into the planet.

She was always excited to help birth a child in Mzee Ng'iti's homestead, as had been the case with his other children, given Ng'iti's stature in the community.

However, this was not to be! By the time the midwife arrived at Mzee Ng'iti's homestead, the baby was already born. And it was a son to boot! Waves of disappointment swept over her for missing out the chance to help deliver Elder Ng'iti's only son, the heir. Even so, she remained upbeat as she came to terms with the reality at hand. And so goes the world, she told herself. Today you get something and tomorrow you do not.

"What you lose on the swings, you gain on the roundabouts," she thought to herself as she shrugged her broad shoulders.

The news of the birth spread like a wildfire in Bogeka. Instant celebrations to welcome the newborn child into a bitter-sweet world increased with each passing second. Meanwhile, painfully dark clouds doubled up on each other in the sky. Readily, a bolt of lightning tore across from the heavens followed by deafening claps of thunder. A curtain of rain came down from the heavens, washing away the sad memories of the many years Mzee Ng'iti's family had struggled to get a male child.

Soon the rains receded and as the sun broke in the horizon in the village of Bogeka, Mzee Ng'iti was singing a new song. His unceasing torments and worries of lacking a heir were history for now. That boy child was named Sakagwa.

It was the custom of the day that the newborn's mother comes outside at the next sunrise and as soon as the sun peeked through distance clouds. On this day, Bochaberi held Sakagwa close to her chest and looked at the rising sun, dazzling its balmy rays, and uttered the typical words spoken when a child was born, "*erioba nderere omwana one*" (sun, watch over and protect my son).

Is that not joy! Praise be to the Lord! Mzee Ng'iti was as happy as a lark. He was satisfied that his sacrifice had not been in vain. You reap what you sow, he told himself. His sacrifice to the gods and his ancestors had been received with open hands.

News of the birth of a male child in Ng'iti's homestead spread like wildfire across all the nooks and crannies in the area. However, there was a mystifying feature about this child that ached the curiosity of the people of Bogeka. The baby boy was born with teeth!

On receiving this news, many people sought to confirm it for themselves. All types of people came!

They were young and old; women and men. All arrived at Mzee Ng'iti's home without delay to witness that unusual event. As the saying of the wise goes, *mwenye macho haambiwi tazama*, one with eyes is never told to look. And indeed, the Danish add that one eye is a better witness than two ears. All desired to confirm that the rare event was not a rumour.

"This is an unusual happening. It has never happened in the history of our community," Elder Nyasende asserted. Mzee Nyasende, a sage in the village, was a man of advanced age, not less than a hundred years old. At the time, he was believed to be the oldest person in Gusii.

This unusual occurrence sparked a heated debate among elders in the community. Some said that such an event was a sign that the child will be of great benefit to the community. Others claimed that it was an ominous sign of calamity that would befall the Abagusii community. Those fearing for the worst sadistically concluded that the child should be killed in order to protect the community from what they dubbed the 'impending great curse'.

Mzee Ng'iti hardly paid attention to the views of this cruel lot. He clearly knew that the torment of the grave is only known by the corpse in it. The bed he had slept in for many years without a son was not a bed of roses. Only he comprehended the agony that came with it. Those advocating for the killing of his son, because of the unusual birth, could not undertand his plight. He promptly dismissed all the blither and blather about his only son. To him, there was nothing more important than the fact that, at last, he had a son, a heir.

He resolved that time was to be the best judge on whether Sakagwa was an ordinary child or not, regardless of people's opinion at the time.

According to Abagusii community customs and traditions, a newborn was named soon after birth. Newborns were given names of the deceased, believing that these dead had been reborn. It was believed that a child named after a morally upright departed person would take after the deceased's virtuous traits. The

desire for good in their children meant that families avoided giving their children names of people believed to have been witches, thieves, murderers, or mentally challenged. They feared that their children might inherit these undesirable traits.

During the naming of a newborn, a number of names would be suggested. One after another, specifically names of people who were of good standing during their lifetime would be mentioned. If the baby sneezed following the mention of a name, it was taken as a confirmation that the baby had accepted that name. Where the baby failed to sneeze, the list of names was repeated until the baby sneezed.

This ritual was followed when naming Mzee Ng'iti's son. Following a rattle of names, the boy sneezed continuously three times once the name "Sakagwa" was mentioned. It prompted gratification! What a joy! Women ululated, *arirririri*, and filled the air with echoes of great excitement.

4. Divinatory Training

Mzee Ng'iti's prayers had been answered. He now had a son. This allowed him to bury past worries and focus on the future. He was beyond excitement. He started making mental notes on how he will teach Sakagwa the art of his herbalist trade when the boy became of age.

Mzee Ng'iti deeply loved his son Sakagwa. The boy was his jewel; the apple of his eye and he needed much care to match this status.

Sakagwa was undisputedly a healthy baby! He was active and in a few months he was already crawling. Years went by and soon Sakagwa was old enough to take care of his father's livestock.

Sakagwa grew up into a morally upright boy. As he matured, he proved to be hard working in every task he undertook. Sometimes, he could go to the bush alone and spend a lot of time thinking and even talking to himself. No one understood why a young boy like him loved to be alone in bushes, forests and even near rivers, thinking and meditating like a prophet.

As years passed and Mzee Ng'iti grew older, his strength declined in tandem. The signs were clear. The man once walked in an upright posture like that of a soldier at a military parade under inspection by a commander-in-chief. Now his waning back had taken a bow-like shape like that of a rainbow. He could neither stand nor walk without the help of a walking stick. He limped on as he walked.

His hair had receded; his baldness becoming more visible and could have been easily mistaken for the

Sahara desert. The little remaining hair on his head had turned from grey to being as white as snow.

Age had caught up with Mzee Ng'iti, what some termed as *being as old as the mountains*. More and more, Ng'iti thought it was time to pass the torch of his trade to his son. He needed to teach his healing skills to Sakagwa.

Despite Sakagwa's young age, Mzee Ng'iti put the boy in tutelage. He took his son along into the forest whenever he went to search for his medicinal ingredients: leaves, roots, and tree barks, among others. He could use these to prepare medicines to treat clients across Gusii and beyond.

Sometimes the duo would spend a whole day in the forest. These were intensive learning sessions for the young lad as Mzee Ng'iti imparted on him knowledge about medicinal plants and the diseases they treated.

"This one is called *omoroka (plectranthus barbatus)*. Its leaves are very effective in treating someone who has a twisted muscle," Ng'iti explained. He would then proceed to explain how it was administered.

"And what of this one?" Sakagwa would ask pointing to another plant.

"Don't touch it. It has a repulsive smell and its leaves sting like a scorpion!" his father would caution.

"And what about that one?"

"Yes...That is a neem tree *(azadirachta indica)*. It is a very important plant. It treats over thirty diseases, including elephantiasis, whooping cough, schistosomiasis, diabetes and many others. If we fail to take care of it, it might become extinct because some people peel its bark carelessly causing it to dry up," Mzee Ng'iti would explain.

"Are the roots of this one edible?"

"Absolutely not! Never eat it! It is very poisonous," Mzee Ng'iti would warn.

At heart, Mzee Ng'iti was pleased with his son's desire to learn and absorb everything in detail. To ensure that Sakagwa understood his teachings, Mzee Ng'iti would test Sakagwa without the son's knowledge. From time to time, he would send him to the forest alone to collect twenty or more herbal medicines of different kinds. The son proved to be good at the tasks. He merited his father's tests and it pleased his father. It gave the Mzee faith that Sakagwa would continue his father's art even after his death.

Perhaps, this was the reason that made Mzee Ng'iti want to hasten bequeathing his son with his herbal expertise, aside from the fact that his days on earth were numbered. It was customary for every father to explain to his son the origin of the Abagusii community in order to emphasize the importance of preserving the community's heritage. This was meant to strengthen the traditions of the community and to pass them on from one generation to another.

As well, these teachings were meant to impart the importance of protecting and conserving trees because they are of great importance in people's lives. This measure initiated a campaign for conserving trees for the benefit of future generations.

Mzee Ng'iti also taught his son how to diagnose different diseases based on their varying symptoms and signs, as explained by those affected. In turn, Sakagwa's good intellectual capacity allowed him to learn extensively from his father.

5. The Origin and Culture of Abagusii

When Sakagwa was about twelve years of age, his father started preparing him for passage to adulthood. Like all boys in the community, Sakagwa needed to go through the mandatory rites of passage. The rituals included extensive education passed down generations of the Abagusii community. In those days, the history of the community was passed from one generation to another orally. Parents usually taught their children at the fireside where discussions and storytelling took place in the evenings after work. Special education and training was also given to young men at special *gesarate* settings where young men of various age groups often lived for designated periods of time.

Based on his life experience, Mzee Ng'iti could tell that things were changing with different generations. Communities were drifting from their indigenous cultures and beliefs. Elders were no longer as keen in teaching their children their cultures and traditions as had been in in his time of groowing up.

Having predicted that in the future the indigenous cultures and traditions of various African communities would be eroded and by foreign cultures, Mzee Ng'iti took it upon himself to teach his children and wives the history and culture of the Abagusii community.

He understood that, whoever does not understand his or her culture is a slave. Mzee Ng'iti could prophecy what would happen in a few years to come. This gift enabled him to determine what could befall some youths, particularly after his generation. They would imitate foreign cultures and ignore those of their communities.

One evening, after the whole family had had supper, Mzee Ng'iti, his wives, his daughters and Sakagwa sat around an open fire. It was unusual for this family to gather together as it was that evening. Therefore, Mzee Ng'iti took advantage of the opportunity to explain to his children the nature of their community and more importantly, its culture and beliefs.

"My dear children," Mzee Ng'iti began. "It is a custom that we inherited from our forefathers that elders are supposed to explain to their children the nature and culture of their communities," he continued as he moved his round three-legged stool a little back from the fire that was now burning furiously after one of his wives fanned it with more firewood. His children, particularly Sakagwa, were very attentive with their eyes fixed at their father. They were eager to know where their community had come from.

"The oral history that has been passed on to us from the ancestors of the ancestors of our ancestors, over many generations tells us that, in ancient times, our community lived in a place that was called *Misri.*"

"In that country, our community was ruled by a wealthy leader with tremendous power called Kintu. According to what we were told, Kintu was the grandfather of the grandfather of the grandfather of Mogusii. Kintu not only ruled the Abagusii, but he also ruled the ancestors of other related ethnic communities such as the Maragoli, the Ganda, the Kikuyu, Embu, Meru and Kuria," Mzee Ng'iti said.

"Why did the Abagusii migrate from Misri?" asked Sakagwa who was sitting next to his father.

"That's a very good question, my son," Mzee Ng'iti said approvingly as he coughed. He then continued, "we are told that a severe drought befell that land and greatly affected their source of livelihood which was livestock. This forced them to leave Misri led by Kintu."

"After leaving Misri, they walked for many days, crossed many mountains and valleys, went through plateaus and crossed rivers. Ultimately, they reached and decided to settle in the area around the present-day Mount Elgon. Here they were hunters of wild animals and gatherers of wild fruits. Among the animals they hunted for food were gazelles, warthogs, antelopes, oryx and even elephants."

"Did our community just depend on hunting animals and gathering fruits?" Nyakerario, Sakagwa's sister, asked.

"No my daughter, they also reared cattle, goats and sheep. Moreover, they grew millet and rice," Mzee Ng'iti explained.

"Then why did they leave the Mount Elgon area?" asked Sakagwa who was now very fascinated with his father's account of the origins of their community.

"Mmmh, yes .... after staying in the Mount Elgon area for a long time, their population grew as their children matured and gave birth to even more children. Soon, pastures for their livestock became inadequate. Due to high population, land grew increasingly scarce. Conflicts over farming land broke out. They decided to leave the area in search of pastures for their livestock as well as larger tracts of land to cultivate. Furthermore, we are told that it is likely that their exodus was caused by attacks from tribes like the Kikuyu, Embu and Mbeere who were also living near Mount Elgon."

"We are told also that the Embu, Kikuyu and Mbeere also ultimately moved from the Mount Elgon area and settled in the Rift Valley and the area now known as Central Province," Mzee Ng'iti said joyfully as he saw his children's genuine interest to know more about their community.

Mzee Ng'iti's wives remained silent for a long time listening attentively to their husband's account. Because Mzee Ng'iti understood that silence means a lot, he decided to give them a chance to also tell their children what they knew about the history of the Abagusii community.

"I have carefully followed your father's narration. I agree with everything he has told you. Perhaps, the only thing he did not tell you is the origin of the name of our ethnic community "Abagusii" or "Gusii'," Bochere said while looking at her husband as if seeking consent to proceed. Mzee Ng'iti nodded in agreement with her statement.

"The name 'Gusii' probably came from two sources. First, it is said that it resulted from the names 'Gwassi' or 'Kosova' which is a place on the shores of Lake Sango, which the British later renamed Lake Victoria. It is believed that the Abagusii lived near that lake for a while after leaving the Mount Elgon area. Second, there are claims also that this name came from 'Mogusii', the ancestor of Abagusii. Mogusii lived up to the end of the 16th century and was the great, great grandson of Kintu who your father told you led the Abagusii out of Misri," Bochere said.

It was now Bochaberi's turn to narrate to Sakagwa and Nyakerario more about their community. She had listened to the discussion for a long time and she agreed with what had already been said. She wanted to add one aspect of faith and culture of that community. Without any hesitation, she began her narration.

"Your father and my co-wife have said almost everything about our community except for the beliefs and customs of our community. Among the Abagusii, there is a strong belief in their God known as *Engoro*. The Abagusii believe that *Engoro* always helped them whenever they were confronted with problems such as hunger and disease and even protected them when they were attacked by their enemies. We still believe that *Engoro* is the one who created the heavens and the earth, the moon, and the stars besides giving us life," Bochaberi said.

"Where did Engoro live?" Sakagwa asked.

Bochaberi thought for a moment while looking at her husband, Mzee Ng'iti, as if she needed help. This was a hard question. When Mzee Ng'iti realized this, he intervened immediately and said, "our fathers told us that he lived in heaven, *Erioba*, near the sun," he said as he looked up into the sky. Everyone looked up and Mzee Ng'iti and burst into laughter. All of them smiled when they were unable to see through the sky.

While Mzee Ng'iti continued to laugh at the way everybody had looked up expecting to see heaven, where *Engoro* lived, Bochaberi proceeded to recount what she knew about the subject she had introduced.

"God, or *Engoro*, and human beings related through the spirits of departed ancestors, C*hisokoro*. The spirits do not have any form. They are like the wind; and they live in the caves at Manga Ridge. That is where we sacrificed to them about twelve years ago and asked them to open for us the doors of grace so that Sakagwa would be born," she said while she stared at Sakagwa who smiled to hear this.

Mzee Ng'iti interrupted his wife's speech and said, "our ancestors who died a long time ago and became spirits, *Chisokoro*, never harm living members of our community without a reason. When it happens, for example when the living neglect to name newborns after them, they become angry and can bring great misfortune. For example, when you were born, we named you 'Sakagwa', one of our ancestor's (*esokoro*'s) name. They bring harm on the living by appearing as ghosts, *Amarengari,* to anyone who fails to fulfil their wishes or by causing calamities such as hunger, disease or even disaster," Mzee Ng'iti emphasized. He stressed the calamities that can befall the community when they rebel against the spirits of their ancestors.

Bochere added, "When it happens that those of us that are alive are affected by these spirits, urgent action must be taken. A diviner, *Omoragori* is the only one capable of discerning the wishes of the ancestors and to give orders on what kind of sacrifices are required to calm the anger of the spirit."

"How can we tell when our ancestors are angry with us?" Sakagwa asked.

"A very good question, my son. Whenever our ancestors are angry with us, you will see the appearance of rare animals such as the pythons and the dreadful sounding owl. In many African societies, an owl is associated with transgression," Mzee Ng'iti explained to Sakagwa.

"Did Mogusii have any children?" asked Nyakerario.

"Ah...yes. It is said that he had six sons. They were known by the names of Nyaribari, Ochoge, Girang'o, Obasi, Getutu and Monchari. These are of course the

fathers of the various Abagusii clans. Nyaribari is the father of Nyaribari clan. Ochoge is the father of the Machoge clan. Obasi is the father of the Basi clan while Getutu is the father of the Kitutu clan. Another clan is the Wanjare, one that was founded by Monchari. Likewise, Mogirango is the father of the Bogirango clan. There are six clans among the Abagusii," Ng'iti explained intensively.

After this satisfactory explanation, Sakagwa and his sister showed signs of content on their faces. They had learnt a lot from these detailed narratives on the culture, customs, beliefs and traditions of their community. Undoubtedly, they also promised to preserve these teachings for the benefit of future generations.

Everybody now looked tired. Children and their parents bade each other goodbye and wished each other good night. Everyone retired to their beds to catch sleep.

6. Mzee Ng'iti's Death

Years passed. Soon Mzee Ng'iti was clocking ninety years of age in the estimation of those who knew him. With this advanced age he started to succumb to the will of nature. Suddenly, disease struck his weakening body. Despite being a proficient herbalist, none of Mzee Ng'iti's medicines could cure him. Indeed, as the saying goes, a doctor does not cure himself. Fortunately, Ng'iti had passed on to Sakagwa the knowledge and expertise of his herbal medicine and the history of Abagusii culture. Now the son became his father's doctor and Sakagwa worked hard to meet his aged father's health and material needs. It is often said that son of a blacksmith who does not live up to expectations will work the bellows or be demoted. It was Sakagwa's turn to treat his father and meet his expectations.

This prompted Sakagwa to start to travel a lot to accomplish the mission at hand - healing his father. His visits to the forest in search of medicinal herbs that could cure his father increased by the day. Nonetheless, *jitihada haiondoi kudura*, effort does not negate destiny. Mzee Ng'iti's ailment was neither responding to the medicine nor the sacrifices offered. As days went by, the old man's health worsened. His eyes sank into their sockets. He shriveled like sun-dried fish and his body became slump. He was on the verge of demise, inching ever steadily to the grave. Poor Elder Ng'iti! He was neither dead nor healthy.

Nevertheless, Sakagwa did not give up! He kept looking for ways to cure his father. One day, he woke up early in the morning even before the first cockcrow. He travelled to a distant forest with the usual aim of finding medicine that could save his father's life.

He wandered around the forest all day looking for different types of plants that he could combine to make the desired medicine, but without success. By the afternoon, Sakagwa was very tired. The sun was unusually hot that day. It angrily shone its rays as if it was on a mission to punish the creatures on earth.

Due to extreme exhaustion, Sakagwa decided to sit under the shade of a tree to rest before setting on his journey back home.

He became overwhelmed with grief whenever he thought of his father's illness. It did not give him a break, during the day or at night. He was worried about what could happen if his father succumbed to the illness.

No sooner had Sakagwa sat in the shade, than he started dozing. He was half-awake and half-asleep. In this state, he heard a terrifying voice singing from afar. He thought that it was a dream. The song went thus:

You woke up at dawn, and entered into the forest,

You searched for medicine, to cure the disease,

And now you are tired, resting in the shade,

Go son go, quickly return home.

All of a sudden, he woke up and looked up on the tree under whose shade he was resting. His eyes met with those of an extremely dark bird, with a round face and big marble-like eyes. Then the bird recited the song twice in a row.

An immediate thought came to his mind! He reckoned that the bird must be an owl. He recollected the story told to him and his sister Nyakerario by their parents. It was that the sight of an owl, or a python in broad daylight, was a sign of bad omen. Where there is smoke, there is usually a fire, the saying goes. Surely, he reasoned, there was trouble ahead.

His heart started beating fast! He felt as if it would to tear open his chest! Suddenly, his fatigue disappeared. He shot to his feet, *twa!* He gathered himself and stretched his body. Feeling energized, he headed straight home.

He started off on the journey home, half running, half walking. About one kilometre from home, he heard screams. This took him by surprise as screams were rare in their homestead. Where there is smoke there is fire, he recalled once more.

"How is dad doing? Is he critically ill? Has he died?" thoughts ran through his mind. He was confused. This made him quicken his pace. He ran as fast as a gazelle; he was panting, and his body became drenched in sweat. The sweat soaked the hide that he was wearing across his shoulder and around his waist.

As he neared the homestead, Sakagwa saw a crowd of people outside their house. This worried him even more. When he got home, he did not ask any questions. Soon an elderly man led him to where his father, Mzee Ng'iti, had been laid down to rest.

Mzee Ng'iti and son were given some privacy by the elders. The two stared at each other in silence. Sakagwa was still panting like an athlete, and dripping with sweat. He wiped his face of sweat with the palm of his left hand. Then he approached his father and caressed the old man's face almost in tears.

Mzee Ng'iti was weak but remained calm. On seeing his son, Mzee Ng'iti smiled as a show of the comfort from his only son whom he loved a lot. He opened his mouth to say something but it was in vain! He was left fumbling. Sakagwa was forced to move closer to his father in order to hear what he was saying.

"I have completed m-my j-jo-journey on earth, mm-y l-last wo-rds are these, you aa-are a wise son, l-lead o-oour pe-people. B-But b-but be-beware of a ce-certain g-g-group of elders that wanted you to be killed soon after you were born…because you were born with teeth!"

This was followed by a long pause before Mzee Ng'iti said the word "goodbye!" Then the old man closed his eyes forever. He never woke up again!

On realizing that his father had died, Sakagwa cried out in anguish. This a cry startled those that were outside his father's room. They knew that the inevitable had come! What they had anticipated since Mzee Ng'iti began to ail had finally happened.

The death of Elder Ng'iti came as a big blow to his family and the many in the community who benefited from his herbal medicines.

A few days later, Mzee Ng'iti was buried with great honour, with people from diverse backgrounds and ethnic groups coming to mourn his death.

The death of Mzee Ng'iti left a big gap in his family, a gap similar to the one left when a whole chapter of a book is ripped out.

Nevertheless, the important thing is that he did not die with the herbal medical knowledge that he possessed. He had passed that knowledge to his son, Sakagwa who was ready to use it, like his father did, for the benefit of the people in his and other ethnic communities. The wheel of that profession would continue rolling into the future.

7. The Puzzle Solved

Soon, the mourning period was over. It was time to move on and Sakagwa chose to look ahead, letting bygones be bygones. His main goal was to create a better future for his people using the advice and knowledge passed on to him by his late father. Despite his young age, Sakagwa was high-minded; he always asked questions with the intent of understanding concepts in good depth.

Sakagwa made a habit of spending time in the tranquility of the forest. Here, he sought refuge and spent time reflecting on the last words his father whispered to him before he died.

He did not understand what his father meant by the words, "I have completed my journey on earth and my advice is this, you are a smart child, lead our people. Be wary of a group of elders who wanted you to be killed when you were born because you were born with teeth. Goodbye!"

These words spoken by his late father troubled him and kept ringing in his head. He decided not rest until he got to the bottom of the issue. He started to search for and find ways to solve the puzzle. As the ancients had said, *fumbo mfumbie mjinga, mwerevu ataling'amua*, puzzles are for fools, the wise will solve them. Sakagwa worked within every possible means to find the meaning in his fathers' words.

His visits to the forest became more frequent. He had to find medicinal herbs for both his nearby and distant clients that visited his home for medical attention.

As time passed, Sakagwa excelled in his profession. His reputation spread throughout Gusii and the neighbouring communities. It went beyond mere use of herbs for treating diseases. He also excelled in other ways. And people developed immense confidence in him as their advisor. For example, in times of calamities like drought, pestilence, and famine, they went to him for counsel. With each passing day, Sakagwa's stature and reputation grew beyond the borders of Abagusii community. He acquired a larger stature and became even more highly regarded than his father.

Unfortunately for Sakagwa, he failed to comprehend that his recognition was a blessing in disguise. His astute reputation earned him a trail of enemies from his community. Driven by envy, a group of elders in the community hatched secret schemes and plots. Cause and reason?

"How can a child who was only born recently gain such fame and become the principal advisor of the community?" They would ask angrily.

The antagonistic elders gave a number of reasons for opposing Sakagwa, including that he was a young man with no experience in life. He did not have any grey hair on his head. Among the Abagusi, grey hair was regarded as a symbol of wisdom and without it, the elders believed, he lacked wisdom. Nonetheless, Sakagwa was exceptional with the gift of wisdom even at a tender age.

For a long time, elders had used the excuse of grey hair to deny young people the opportunity to lead in various sectors of society. Sakagwa proved them wrong. Clearly, even young people could give beneficial advice to the society.

These elders hated Sakagwa because he always spoke the truth. The pain we enjoy putting on others is unbearable when put on us! Sakagwa's forthrightness did not settle well with a section of elders.

At one time, there was a consistent pattern of drought and famine in the community. Some in the sought Sakagwa's counsel regarding these calamities. His response to them was that *Engoro* was not happy with the whole community because it was not keeping its traditions as required, adding that, "majority of the elders among you never offer sacrifices to our ancestors".

A section of the elders were not pleased with this response from Sakagwa. They thought that he was insane, ill-mannered, and disrespectful to them as elders of the community.

Instead of taking Sakagwa's warning seriously, this section of elders disregarded his advice and intensified their brawl with him. They plotted to kill him. They hired thugs to attack him at his home in the night.

As the saying goes, walls have ears!

Rumours of the plot to kill Sakagwa spread like bush fire across the community. When it came to his attention, he alerted his family of the looming danger. In secrecy, they all fled and sought refuge in a nearby village of Mwamosioma. When the hired gangsters came to Sakagwa's home, he was nowhere to be seen. In anger, they torched all houses in Mzee Ng'iti's compound.

The viciousness of the raid startled Sakagwa and became an eye-opener for him. He came to terms with his father's puzzling advice of being cautious of a certain group of elders.

In spite of hostilities from these elders, Sakagwa was neither scared nor discouraged. He defended his mettle to criticize his community when the need arose. He was especially concerned about the constant warfare between the Kitutu and Wanjare clans. He warned them that their civil war weakened the Gusii community and that such weakness could pave way for the neighbouring Luo, Kipsigis and Maasai ethnic communities to easily defeat them during war.

"Why don't you understand that unity is strength?" Sakagwa would ask.

When he realized that some elders did not pay attention to his advice only because of his age, he gave out a second warning to his people. He foretold that they would face disastrous famine if they did not heed his advice. He prophesied that the Gusii region would be invaded by a cloud of locusts that would destroy all of their crops and cause famine.

On hearing this, his opponents dismissed him as a day dreamer. They called him a traitor, termed him heretic, and branded him insane. But, in his heart, Sakagwa understood that it is better to make hay while the sun shines. Disaster was on the way. Moreover, as the Kiswahili saying goes, *lisemwalo lipo, na kama halipo litakuja*, that which is spoken of is present and if it is not, it will come to pass.

8. The Great Calamity

Three years passed before Sakagwa's prophecy came to pass. A swarm of locusts invaded the land of Abagusii destroying all the crops in the farms and any plant life in sight. The land was laid bare! It was followed by a fierce drought the following year. In that time the land became so dry that hundreds of wild beasts, especially elephants, could be seen wandering in search of food and water. Then the inevitable happened, there was a devastating calamitous famine which led to deaths of many people, livestock and wildlife.

The famine was so grave that people were forced to live on leaves of any plants they came across. To this day, elders talk about that great famine that was termed *Enchara ya Amakongiro*. It was named after a local drought resistant plant that people subsisted on during the duration of the drought. As if that were not enough, a devastating animal disease hit with vengeance wiping out most of the livestock that had survived the drought.

Abagusii women bore the brunt of the pain and suffering. The situation compelled some of them to trade their children for food from their Kipsigis and Luo neighbours. In most cases it was the only means of saving their lives and those of their children.

On the other hand, the Maasai and Kipsigis intensified cattle rustling forays against the Abagusii. Weakened by famine and diminished food sources, the Abagusii community became susceptible to attacks and was unable to defend itself from the frequent raids.

The fulfilment of Sakagwa's prophecy became an epiphany for those that were opposed to him. They decided to look for a solution to the calamity at hand. Led by Elder Ogaro, they came to Sakagwa and pleaded with him to offer them a solution to the series of disasters that had befallen the community.

"Thousands and thousands of our livestock have died. Many of our children have been sold to other communities. Our people are dying from hunger, diseases, and from the sharp spears of the Kipsigis. Does *Engoro* and our ancestors want our community to perish?" the elders complained to Sakagwa.

"When I told you that these things will happen, you turned your ears away. You claimed that I was insane and a day dreamer. Do you remember that?" Sakagwa asked them.

The elders looked down in great shame. Others wished the ground could crack open and swallow them alive. If regret were a horn, one's horn would reach the sky.

Only if they had heeded Sakagwa's warning without scoffing at his young age, the community would not have suffered all those calamities.

"Go back home. Give me until tomorrow to meditate over what needs to be done," Sakagwa told them.

After elder Ogaro and his group left, Sakagwa gathered his divine paraphernalia and disappeared into the forest near Manga Ridge. He spent the night there consulting his ancestors. When that group of elders returned to his home the next day, he told them to accompany him to the graves of their forefathers, Oisera and Nyakundi, where they offered a sacrifice.

Besides that sacrifice, Sakagwa advised the elders to follow the customs and traditions of the community. He also directed them to regularly offer sacrifices to their ancestors as had been the custom over generations.

On that day, it rained heavily, accompanied with the rustling sounds of thunder. Some of the elders remembered that heavy rain also fell when Sakagwa was born. Surely, there was something divine about this man.

For the next four years, there were bumper harvests of food. Families filled their granaries with harvests of bulrush (pearl) millet, finger millet, sorghum and even cassava. The term 'famine' soon became distant in the people's memory.

The elders realised that Sakagwa's knowledge and wisdom were of benefit to the entire community. They quickly made him their chief advisor. This action dismissed the previously held and foolish claim that it is only grey-haired elders who were endowed with wisdom.

* * *

Sakagwa opened a new chapter in the leadership of his community. He had demonstrated that, despite his young age, the gift that he had been graced with was of great value to the community. Now the elders sought his counsel severally as a chief advisor.

Soon, Sakagwa built his house outside his late father's compound and continued to serve the community in his new role. Consequently, Sakagwa's prominence grew with each passing day.

At one time, the people of his clan were troubled by the constant attacks from the Isiria Maasai. The elders of Mugirango clan appointed a delegation led by Elder Nyabwanga Omingo to seek guidance from Sakagwa.

When they got to his home, they found him sitting on his father's three legged round stool under the shade of a tree shade in front of his house. In his hand, he had his "L-shaped" staff and a fly whisk.

"I greet you my elders," Sakagwa respectfully greeted the elders and invited them to sit.

"We greet you, our son," they answered as they sat down.

"How is everything at home?"

"There is no peace; we face daily warfare. We don't even get a wink of sleep," one elder with white hair replied.

"The Isiria Maasai are always fighting us. We have no peace at all," Elder Nyabwanga added.

"How can I be of help?" asked Sakagwa.

"We want guidance from you on how to deal with these enemies," answered elder Nyabwanga.

Sakagwa stood up slowly and walked a short distance away from where the elders were seated. He seemed lost in deep thoughts. Intermittently, he could be heard talking to himself. Soon after, he returned to the gathering and took his seat. The elders were attentive, anxiously waiting for his pronouncement.

"Go back to your homes and look for a black goat with one breast," he said. "When you find it, bury it alive. Once you do that, you will always defeat your enemies," he added.

The elders were dumbfounded to hear that. They thought that Sakagwa was insane to give them such advice. Nevertheless, they had no option but to do as advised. They returned home and begun searching for a black goat with one breast.

They looked for it desperately among goats across the six clans of the Abagusii community. They crisscrossed Machoge, Kitutu, Nyaribari, and Bonchari clans without any success.

When they were about to give up, they got information that a goat of that nature had been found in the clan of Bobasi. Even so, it was difficult to get the goat because the Bobasi and Mugirango clans were not in good terms. Each clan thought of itself as being superior to the other. However, the Mugirango clan had to do the necessary. They were forced to part with two oxen in exchange of the rare goat.

On getting the goat, elders of Mugirango clan proceeded as instructed by Sakagwa. They buried it alive. Later when they went to war against the Maasai in the battle of *Ntomocha*, "no room for failure," they fought hard and secured a great victory. It was a consequential win because for the few years that followed, the Maasai did not have the courage to provoke the people of Mugirango again. This victory further cemented Sakagwa's reputation as a seer and enhanced his respect in his community.

9. Unity is Strength

With each new day, Sakagwa's fame spread far and wide. In addition to his sound advice, many people, including elders from all of the Abagusii clans, realised that the herbal remedies that he gave to treat various diseases were authentic. It became evident that his advice to Mugirango clan had come to fruition. It had earned the clan many more successes in their war against the Maasai. Consequently, an elder from the Kitutu clan, Gori Kimaiga, led another delegation to Sakagwa's home at Seusi.

The aim of the trip was to discuss, at length, the frequent attacks that the people of his area had suffered in the hands of the neighbouring Kipsigis.

"What can we do to ensure that our homes, children and wealth are safe when we are attacked by the Kipsigis?" Kitutu clan elders asked him.

Sakagwa was not one to offer quick answers or jump into conclusions. Even at his relatively tender age, he really loved to investigate the problems facing the people before pronouncing himself. He did this by being alone in the forest where he spent a lot of time thinking and reflecting on various issues and challenges facing his community.

He realised that the biggest problem facing the community was lack of unity amongst the Abagusii clans of Kitutu, Wanjare, Mugirango, Nyaribari, Bobasi and Machoge. Elder Kimaiga and his fellow elders were afraid that if the Abagusii were not prepared, the Kipsigis would attack, defeat, and rob them of their land and livestock.

At that time, whenever two ethnic communities fought, the defeated community was forced to move elsewhere and its land forfeited to the winners of the conflict.

On listening to the various complaints and fears of the clans, Sakagwa decided to convene a major conference involving all the clans. A few days later, elders from the clans of Mugirango, Kitutu, Machoge, Nyaribari and Bobasi arrived at Sakagwa's home to attend this exclusive meeting. Such a meeting had never been held before in Gusii. At the meeting, Sakagwa listened to various opinions of the elders from all corners of Gusii concerning the problems they were facing with raids from neighbouring ethnic groups.

Finally, he responded eloquently to the elders' concerns showing a lot of respect and wisdom.

"My elders the toe is a small part of the body. But you understand that when it gets hurt, the whole body will be in pain. Right?" Sakagwa asked.

"Yes you are right," the elders answered in unison.

"Therefore, after carefully listening to your views, I have realized that we have one serious problem among our clans; we are not united. Every clan sees itself as better than the other. For example, the Bomachoge clan feels superior to the Bobasi clan. In the same way Mugirango clan feels superior to the Kitutu clan. Don't you know that unity is strength and division is weakness?" he asked, to which the elders nodded in agreement.

"Second, we lack an army that can protect us whenever we are attacked. Therefore, I recommend that we create our own army, *Chinkororo*. Young men

should be trained on military tactics and how to use military weapons including the *amatimo* (spears), *amata* (bows), *chinsara* (arrows), *chinguba* (shields), *chinduruche* (slingshots), and many others..." the elders hailed him with thunderous shouts of joy.

Once the elders' cheering stopped, Sakagwa continued, "three, let's be alert at all times. As soon as enemies from another ethnic community are spotted on our land, an alarm using *ebitureri* (curved animal horns) needs to be raised immediately to signal our army to confront the enemies. Any question up to this point?"

One elder stood up and said, "Sakagwa son of Ng'iti, a young man who was born recently with teeth! Thunder and lightning filled the air when you were born and many of us knew that you were not ordinary. Is that not so fellow elders?" he asked as he coughed and eventually spit out a heavy lump of yellow phlegm.

"Eeeeeh! That's absolutely true," the elders responded in unison.

"Enhee... I would like the elders who plotted to kill Sakagwa in his infancy to come forward publicly and apologize right here."

There was silence like that in a vacuum, creating an overwhelming sense of emptiness.

"Again, I appeal to those who ordered gangsters to attack our late fellow elder Mzee Ng'iti's homestead to come forward and publicly apologize."

Many elders looked down in great shame and observed a deafening silence.

"Why the silence? Remember that when a person mentions dry wood bones in the presence of an old woman, she often becomes uncomfortable and gets offended. When a person describes the state of bones as being dry and weak for example in the presence of an old woman, she often feels hurt. Since you began to quarrel, you have no choice but to end it – be responsible for your actions. The time to face the consequences of your actions is now. It is an opportunity that you need to use to ask Sakagwa for forgiveness for the evils you did to him," the elder insisted.

Sakagwa who was attentively listening to the elder's speech stood up and intervened, "My dear elders, it is important that we forget the past and focus on solving the problems that are ahead of us. I am willing to make peace with you, at the right time – but not now. For now, let's find ways of dealing with the enemies that have been haunting our community," he committed.

The elders nodded their heads in agreement with Sakagwa's views. He then sat down.

Elder Kimaiga from the Kitutu clan stood up and asked, "what we know is that Sakagwa has demonstrated the gift of prophecy. Now can you tell us when the Kipsigis will attack us so that we can be prepared to deal with them?"

This did not go well with his fellow elders who scoffed at him.

"My elders, please don't mock him. Everyone has a right to ask anything here, whether good or bad, be it a good or an absurd question – everyone is worthy of respect." Sakagwa pointed out. "To answer elder Kimaiga, I can say that it is better to be ready at all times and to expect attacks from our enemies at any time," he ended as the elders clapped for him in unison

10. The Battle of Saosao

Sakagwa's recommendation concerning the formation of a youth army (*Chinkororo*) to protect the Abagusii community was received with open arms. Working with Elder Omweno Saka, a prominent herbalist in his own right, from the Bomachoge clan, Sakagwa selected young men from all of the Abagusii clans for military training.

To become a member of *Chinkororo* a young man was required to fulfil certain conditions set by Sakagwa and Elder Omweno Saka. One such condition, among many others, was that when captured by the enemy, one had to die alone. One was not allowed to reveal any information about any member of the group.

Also, a perason joining *Chinkororo* especially voluntarily meant signing up for the service forever. He was not allowed to leave except by death. The final requirement of joining *Chinkororo* was to take an oath to dutifully and wholeheartedly protect the community without prejudice, fear or favouritism.

Soon, Sakagwa who was serving as the military commander of that group had enough members to launch military training in the part of Bomachoge region that now borders Trans Mara region.

Chinkororo, under Sakagwa's leadership prepared adequately to deal with any enemy that would dare to provoke the community. Years passed without anyone attacking Abagusii. However, there came a time when a cattle disease, o*ng'ong'o*, broke out and killed many Luo, Abagusii, and Kipsigis livestock. An infected animal became blind and eventually died.

The Kipsigis, realizing the extent to which their livestock had been depleted, plotted ways to get more cattle. They conspired to attack the Abagusii and Luo communities in order to take away these communities' remaining cattle. The Kipsigis army, led by Arap (son of) Makiche, left from the current area of Sotik. They joined forces with another group from Belgut led by Cheseng'eny Kaborok.

Given his powers of prophecy, Sakagwa had anticipated the looming attack and prepared his army well for it. The Kipsigis army left Sotik early one morning and made it to the southeast bank of River Gucha at sunset. As they continued with plans on launching their attack, a group of vultures fluttered over them. This came to them as a bolt from the blue. It is believed that the vultures were sent by Sakagwa to terrify the invading Kipsigis warriors. To the warriors, this was a bad omen. They feared that it would bring them bad luck.

The wake of vultures terrified Cheseng'eny Kaborok of Belgut. He advised his colleague, Arap Makiche, against going ahead with their plans of invading the Abagusii community. The birds portended a misfortune for them.

Kaborok's army, on hearing this, threatened to banish him on the claim that he was a coward and traitor. On the other hand, the army under the command of Arap Makiche launched an attack on the Abagusii of Mugirango clan, continuing their conquest all the way to Manga. The attack was very successful. Many Abagusii villages were torched and razed to the ground. The grass-thatched and mud-walled houses readily yielded to the fire like tinder. The dry

grass-thatched roofs fuelled the fire, enhancing the fire's rapid spread. The roaring fire from the burning houses formed clouds of smoke that engulfed the air and spread into the skies.

The thick air was also filled with ear-splitting screams and heart-rending wails from girls and women getting abducted by the raiders. The young, strong and energetic invaders not only abducted women and girls, they also drove away livestock – goats and cattle. Sheep were not spared either. The invaders aimed at thoroughly plundering the Abagusii villages and ensuring that nothing was left behind.

Old adage has it that too much of anything can turn poisonous. Woe unto them that fail to realize when they have exceeded limits. Soon, things started going astray for the Kipsigis raiders on reaching Manga.

Malabun Arap Makiche and Kaborok started fighting between themselves over the leadership of the group. Truly, *nahodha wawili chombo huenda mrama,* with two captains the ship loses direction. Disagreements among the two leaders became their undoing. The tug of war between the two led to a great division between their followers.

Makiche and his army chose to go and attack the Luos while Cheseng'eny and his group went their own way. While one of the Kipsigis groups was busy attacking the Luos, drums and trumpets of war were sounded throughout Gusii. Since it was clear that the Kipsigis raiders had gone to plunder the Luo, top runners from the clans of Kitutu, Nyaribari, Mugirango, and Wanjare were sent to apprise *Chinkororo* about the attack.

As soon as they got the message, *Chinkororo* went up to the Manga hills. There, they hid in the forest in readiness for the time when the enemies would pass through the area.

Early in the morning, the Luo community raised an alarm about being attacked and started to drive away their Kipsigis enemies. The Kipsigis army was soon overpowered by Luo warriors because of their small numbers due to division following the differences between their leaders. They fled through the path of Manga hills. Abagusii army was strategically placed in the forested area waiting for the retreating Kipsigis army. Near the Charachani River, while descending the Manga hills, the Kipsigis warriors were taken by surprise by *Chinkororo* who brutally massacred them.

By uniting against their common enemy, the Abagusii and Luo communities killed many Kipsigis raiders and dumped their bodies into the Charachani River. The bleeding bodies discoloured water in the river to a bruising red colour.

It became a matter of survival for some of the Kipsigis fighters as they tried to camouflage with the bushes near the river only to be flushed out by *Chinkororo*. Others pretended to be dead by covering themselves with the branches of shrubs, but to no avail! The Abagusii fighters meticulously foiled their plans and speared them to death.

The Abagusii who had never won any war against their enemies could not believe that they had actually won, especially against the brutal Kipsigis warriors. They branded that battle as the *Battle of Saosao*.

Many of them admitted that if it had not been for Sakagwa's planning and robust preparations, they could not have scored that victory. Sakagwa had finally united the Abagusii community.

11. The Farewell Party

Following the Battle of Saosao, Sakagwa prepared a feast to acknowledge warriors who participated in that battle and elders from the six Abagusii clans. He would also use this to stress the importance of unity in the community.

That opportunity also offered Sakagwa the chance to deliver important prophecies on future events. He believed that there was a limit to success. He did not want disunity and superiority contests to sink his now awakened community that had triumphed over its enemies.

Preparations for that feast were unprecedented. The big day finally came. It was a Friday. God blessed it the same way He had blessed the other days.

Sakagwa had slaughtered a very big bull for his guests, in addition to various food delicacies that had been prepared. Likewise, the host prepared big pots of *busaa*, a traditional brew, for the community elders.

In the feasting, however, the young men that were serving in the community army (*Chinkororo*) were not allowed to drink alcohol. Indeed, aside from rules laid down for the army, it was taboo for young people to drink alcohol. The Abagusii community was aware of the negative effects of alcohol on young people. They were expected to be the leaders of the future and alcohol could derail these expectations.

Any young man that violated this rule was severely punished when caught. In addition to the punishment, any young man who got drunk was heavily fined and prevented from participating in any community protection activities.

On the appointed day, guests began arriving one after another at Sakagwa's homestead starting from nine o'clock in the morning. As guests arrived, those that had come earlier were welcomed to sit under the shade of a giant tree in front of Sakagwa's house.

A procession of dogs, great friends to the homestead dog Simba, were also seen wandering from one end of the compound to the other as they waited for their turn to chew the bones which, of course, were going to be plenty.

A few hours later, the whole homestead was filled with guests. Entertainment was graced by various traditional dances. Women performed *ribina* (a female-led rain dance) as a male band sang *emeino* (traditional Gusii songs usually sang by men) and played *obokano* (a traditional eight stringed music instrument). The young men, on the other hand, showcased their strength in a wrestling competition, *enyameni*, involving the six clans of Abagusii community.

With the entertainment over, it was time to start eating. The guests assaulted their hunger with the various foods that were available. Among the foods were *ugali* made of millet flour, *ugali* made of sorghum flour, *chinsaga* (spider flower, bitter vegetables eaten in the Gusii community) and *amanagu* (black night shade), pumpkins, sweet potatoes, and *obosontoto* (tasty watery seasoning made from animal bile that elders in this community use to eat with roast meat).

There was also plenty of sour milk and goat meat. It was a great feast of historic proportions. To this day,

it is still mentioned by some elders in the Abagusii community.

After eating to their fill, the elders sat around a big pot of beer with each elder's long arched straw dipped into the beer pot. They had gathered to discuss many sensitive community issues.

While they enjoyed the drinking, Sakagwa stood up as the elders cheered him. He cleared his throat and began to speak,

"*Engoro*, God, who made heaven and earth, has given us life and health, and gave us the secret of victory against our enemies, we ask you to be with us until we get to the end of this meeting."

The elders gazed at him as they nodded their heads and marvelled at the gift of eloquence that this young man had been endowed with.

"Elders, are you there?"

"Yes we're."

"Youths, are you thereeee?"

"Yes, we areeeeeee!"

"Our mothers, are you thereeeeee?"

"Yes, we areeeee!!" they replied as they shouted in jubilation.

"I invite you all to this celebration whose aim is to congratulate and honour our young men for the good work they did in defeating our enemies during the Battle of Saosao..." His speech was interrupted by thunderous applause and joyous clapping.

"We have suffered in the hands of other ethnic communities for many years. These other communities have been tossing us around, up-down, left-right, back and forth, like a kite swayed by rogue wind. Now we've discovered the secret to victory. Unityyyy!"

"Unity, unity, unityyy!!" The crowd roared with joy and hand claps.

"Where we have come from is far, and the journey that is ahead of us is also long, discouraging, and full of obstacles," Sakagwa paused briefly, pushed back his round, three-legged stool and picked up his staff, which he had laid on the ground next to him.

"I have been shown by the spirits of our ancestors that in our land, there will come visitors resembling butterflies and they will take our land and displace us."

Sakagwa's words were like stabbing a knife into people's chests. Elder Nyabwanga from Mugirango clan stood immediately and interrupted Sakagwa, "when will they come, for what purpose, and from where?"

"Please, ask your questions later. Give me a chance to deliver to you the message I received from our ancestors...eeh....eeh... The butterflies will grab our land. But, do not dare to fight them. If you do, they will hurt you with their fire-belching sticks," Sakagwa said as he showed them his stick.

"Secondly, these butterflies will bring a giant iron snake to our land. The snake will be belching smoke," Sakagwa concluded his remarks and allowed the elders to ask him questions.

Elder Angwenyi, the leader or Omogambi from the clan of Kitutu stood up and asked, "these people that look like butterflies, where will they come from?"

"They will come from far countries," Sakagwa answered.

"Why will they come to our region," asked Kimaiga.

"I am not sure why, but they might come to build their economies and exploit our labour," Sakagwa answered him.

"You said that it would be dangerous to fight them. Should we just sit back and let them take our land?" Elder Ogaro asked.

"It would be dangerous to fight them because they will have deadly fire-breathing sticks."

Sakagwa also uttered mysterious words in Ekegusii language, "a*mandegere name Getembe, ore n'abamura* *nayae* -- mushrooms will blossom at Getembe (modern Kisii town), only those with strong youngsters will harvest them."

Elder Ogaro tried to interrogate Sakagwa about the meaning of this phrase but Sakagwa answered inaudibly and minced his words – perhaps because of fatigue.

When the question and answer session ended, the guests began to leave one by one. Nevertheless, there are some elders who decided to remain at Sakagwa's homestead to continue drinking and talking. One of them was elder Angwenyi. When midnight came, he bade farewell to his colleagues and went his way.

12. The "Death" of Sakagwa

Elder Angwenyi had just arrived at his home after attending the memorable feast at Sakagwa's home. It was past midnight. The moon lit the sky and a few stars shone like gold. It was extremely quiet. Elder Angwenyi staggered as he walked. He was drunk.

Although he was tired, Angwenyi lit his smoking pipe as soon as he entered his house. Eventually, he sat back and took two to three puffs as he contemplated about Sakagwa's speech at the just ended celebrations.

From their past experiences, elders had learnt to trust and respect Sakagwa. This dated back to the time of the locust invasion and famine which established Sakagwa as a renowned seer in the community.

"…in our land, there will come people that look like butterflies… and they will take our land…do not dare fight them, lest they hurt you with their fire-belching sticks," Angwenyi recalled Sakagwa's words.

"Is it possible for a stranger to intrude into your home and grab your land while you just watch him and do nothing about it? We will fight those butterflies," Angwenyi thought as he puffed out smoke from his mouth, smoke tendrils escaping through his nostrils.

Not long after, unusual screams interrupted Elder Angwenyi's thoughts. He stepped outside to find out where the screams were hailing from as his mind went into a rhetoric spin.

"Could it be an attack by the enemies they had defeated at the recent Battle of Saosao?"

When the screams persisted, Elder Angwenyi dashed back into his house with lightning speed. He set aside his smoking pipe, reached under his bed, took his two spears and ran towards the main entrance of his compound.

On further reflection, he decided not to leave his compound. He was too drunk and tired and in no condition to fight. He went back into his house and continued to smoke his pipe. He puffed severally and decided to go to sleep even though the screams really frightened him.

The cries and screams were still raging the following morning. It was clear that something serious had happened at Sakagwa's home. But what was it about?

Elder Angwenyi and other clan elders were feasting at Sakagwa's home the night before. No one was reported to be sick or unwell in any way at the feast. Why the screams then? This question continued to be a great riddle to him.

By eight in the morning, all corners of the Gusii and beyond had received the tragic news of the "death" of Sakagwa. People began to stream to Sakagwa's home from around nine o'clock in the morning. They formed a mammoth crowd of diverse people in the homestead. There were so many people that there was hardly room for standing or even spitting.

Thousands of women painfully mourned Sakagwa. Even men could not restrain themselves. This is even in the face of traditions of many communities in Africa that did not permit men to express their feelings openly during tragedies. The men were seen shedding tears and blowing their noses discreetly. Most could not hold back their tears.

The dogs that had gathered in the homestead to sponge on the bones from the previous day's feast barked endlessly, like never before. The other livestock, especially cows, seemed to be saddened by this tragedy.

The Luo community from Gem, Mumbo, and Nyakach came to Sakagwa's home in great numbers. They were extremely armed in case Abagusii turned and attacked them. There was no doubt that this community came to pay its last respect to a seer and healer whose services knew no boundaries or ethnic community.

Even the Isiria Maasai came. And so did the Kipsigis, who were defeated by the Abagusii in the Battle of Saosao, to witness the misfortune that had befallen a healer that they valued and respected for his medical services and advice.

From seven to nine o'clock in the morning, elders from the six Gusii clans, once again gathered under the same tree where they had sat the previous day during the party. Many had left for their homes after the party only to return on receiving the sad news.

This time round, they were not gathering to celebrate, but to mourn. It was strange how a buoyant celebration mood rapidly transitioned into mourning without a warning.

These elders were discussing a sensitive issue that roused emotions and anger among the mourners, from various backgrounds and regions, that had come to the home.

It happened that mourners who arrived at Sakagwa's home soon after they got the tragic news found that Sakagwa had already been 'buried'.

The Luos, Maasai, and Kipsigis who came to comfort the Abagusii community and Sakagwa's family, strongly condemned this move as very shameful and

unusual. They were disappointed that they had no chance to pay their last respects to a great man.

"How can such an eminent leader, healer, and seer who is esteemed throughout Gusii land and even among other ethnic communities be buried as quickly as a carcass of a mongrel? How can a leader of such stature be buried so carelessly without any official burial ceremonies as dictated by traditions which he fought for in his entire life?" one old man asked.

In addition to being 'buried' in an incomprehensible manner, another riddle soon arose. This was in connection with the 'grave' in which Sakagwa was allegedly buried. It appeared to be as small as that of a little child.

Fortunately, as the wise say, where there are wise elders nothing goes wrong. Therefore, under the chairmanship of Elder Angwenyi, the elders decided to exhume Sakagwa's body immediately so that it could be buried afresh according to customs and with honours befitting such a respected seer and healer.

Without wasting time, the elders ordered young men to the task who gathered tools for exhuming Sakagwa's body. They removed their hide skin clothing and remained bare-chested. Soon, they started digging Sakagwa's 'grave' while throwing out soil like moles.

They dug, dug, and dug. They dug up the grave until their bodies got soaked in sweat. Those who got thirsty were given water to drink before continuing with the excavation. It was extreme hard work!

They dug to a depth of approximately fifteen feet where they found the round three-legged stool that Sakagwa loved to sit on. This is the stool that he always carried wherever he went to attend meetings of the council of elders. Indeed, he had sat on the same stool during the feast of the previous day.

Undeterred, the young men kept digging. The more they dug and removed soil from the grave, the more its depth increased along with the hopes of getting to Sakagwa's body. After another fifteen feet, the young men who were now panting from the heavy work, found Sakagwa's rod.

The recovery of the seat and rod was a sign that they were not far from their goal of getting to the seer's body. They hastened their speed and they continued to dig as the elders waited anxiously to see Sakagwa's body.

When they got to the bottom of that 'grave', they found the head of the bull that was slaughtered for the feast celebrating the victory of Battle of Saosao the day before.

This situation provoked a lot anxiety and fear. Old and young, women and men, visitors and locals, were all left dumb-founded with shock. Fear was written all over their faces as their eyes popped out. People gathered in small groups. In low tones they discussed this shocking happening. Truly, as it is said, if you marvel at small things just know that there are still big things you have not seen. Most of them thought they had seen shocking things before; the mystery of Sakagwa's death beat them all. More shocking things were still waiting for them.

This puzzling event brought about different thoughts among elders as they tried to explain and solve it. There are those who claimed that the family of Sakagwa was playing games with them by lying to people that Sakagwa had died.

However, those who followed his life and its dynamics carefully wondered whether there was a possibility that Sakagwa had really died and then turned into a spirit and joined his ancestors in the next world.

Eerie thoughts surrounding the episode frightened many mourners. Fearing possible confrontation with the spirits of their ancestors, they fled.

However, such reasoning did not satisfy many people. Did Sakagwa really die or was he killed by his relatives who then hid his body fearing the wrath of the whole Abagusii community?

And if Sakagwa did not die, how come his seat, his rod, and the head of the bull that was slaughtered at his farewell banquet were found in his 'grave'? Who dug such a small and extremely deep "grave" for him? And if truly Sakagwa had died and joined his ancestors, what was the reason for leaving them with the three items?

13. Sakagwa's Ghost

Two years after Sakagwa's 'death', the British began to arrive in Africa and made Uganda part of their colonial territory.

The colonised territory included a significant spread of Nyanza Province.

British officers from the King's African Rifles (K.A.R.) battalion arrived in Gusii armed with deadly weapons.

Soon, Abagusii community elders realized that these uninvited visitors had come to occupy their land. They sounded an alarm and called for an emergency meeting that was attended by elders from all six Abagusii clans.

It is said that a trumpet is never blown without a good reason for doing so. The elders held a meeting, under the leadership of Elder Angwenyi, to discuss the arrival of 'white people' on their land.

"The aim of this meeting is to discuss how we will deal with these intruders who have taken over our land," elder Angwenyi remarked on opening the discussions.

"What you have said is true. But remember that the 'late' Sakagwa warned us not to dare provoke them, otherwise they will hurt us with their fire-belching sticks!" one elder noted.

"Sakagwa is no longer with us now. Out of sight out of mind. What is more realistic is to use our youth army, *Chinkororo*, to deal with these foreigners. Our ancestors, *Chisokoro*, will never be pleased with us if we don't find fight for our land," Elder Angwenyi reiterated.

After discussions in that and other subsequent meetings, it was resolved that it would be an act of cowardice if the Abagusii community failed to come forth to defend their rights. "We can't sit back and just watch," they remarked.

Soon after encamping in the Gusii region, the British decided to build their administrative headquarters in Gusii. This move greatly angered the local people who began to resist it, tooth and nail.

Chinkororo took it as a duty and led in defending the rights of their community. However, their efforts were not successful. The British attacked them with guns that fired bullets and killed many fighters from the community. The colonizers burned down homes, destroyed food crop fields, and took away large numbers of livestock.

Soon the situation became unbearable. The elders urged all circumcised young men to marry and sire children for fear that the British would wipe out an entire generation. While doing so, they remembered Sakagwa's counsel on the coming of the "white man" before his death'.

Meanwhile, British attacks against Abagusii intensified day by day. They did not spare the secured grazing camps, *ebisarate*, where they continued to rob local inhabitants of their livestock.

When they could no longer endure the aggravation and harassment of the "white visitors", Abagusii decided to defend their rights and interests by all means possible.

One of the young men who were aggravated by the acts of violence committed by the British, was Otenyo

Nyamaterere. Otenyo had a baby girl named Bosibori and he lived with his aunt called Moraa.

Moraa was also a prominent healer and respected prophetess among the Abagusii community. She too was tired of the cruelty of the British against Abagusii.

"What kind of visitor is this? Instead of submitting and asking us to welcome him to our land, he wants to take it over by force," Moraa complained.

"By God I have run out of patience. I will teach these visitors a lesson, even though the elders have warned us that their fire-belching sticks are a mortal danger to us. We cannot sit by and allow this white visitor to sit on our heads and oppress us as he desires. We are certainly not his puppets," Otenyo spurred.

Otenyo did not believe in words. He wanted actions. Through the encouragement of some elders and his aunt, Moraa, Otenyo assembled some of his fellow young men who served in the *Chinkororo* army.

"It's our time now to retaliate against these strangers who are irritating us day by day," Otenyo told them.

"What you are saying is true," added one fighter with a large head and squinting eyes.

"Moreover, Moraa will give us medicine that will shield us against the bullets of the enemy."

"Men fight one on one," said another.

After holding several meetings and training in secret, Otenyo and his group were ready to deal with the British.

***

Preparations for battle were now complete. The day for battle came. Otenyo and his group woke up at cockcrow.

Before leaving for war, Otenyo and his squad of warriors lined up prepared to receive Moraa's medicine. She administered it on them one by one. She sprinkled more on their chests with a flywhisk. Moraa did this while chanting in an incomprehensible language. Once the whole army had received medicine, Moraa raised her flywhisk and said in a deep voice, "go like the wind – to the north, south, east and west. Be shielded and deal with the 'red soil' like real men."

The squad was armed to the teeth. They carried their well sharpened spears. On their shoulders hang bows.

Their poison arrows were in quivers on their backs. They left in a procession at daybreak.

The warriors had learnt that British officers had planned an attack in the Manga area. The foreigners would rob the residents of their livestock. Therefore, Otenyo and his group used shortcuts and got to the Manga area ahead of the invaders. They hid in bushes.

The sun had started to rise. Its brown rays made the Gusii highlands, which were covered by a blanket of green plants, shine like gold.

A few clouds, that were as white as cotton, were noticeable in the sky above them. A light wind blew, causing tree branches to whistle and produce unique gentle music.

That calmness was interrupted suddenly. Otenyo and his group spotted British officers approaching their hideout.

The warriors tiptoed and crawled forward like sweet potato plants. Some of them held their spears in readiness position while others placed their arrows on their bows and got ready to attack.

A while passed before the British officers came close to where Otenyo and his colleagues were hiding. At the front of the convoy was Mr. Geoffrey Alexander Northcote. The elders of the Abagusii community called him "Nyarigoti" because they could not pronounce his real name "Northcote."

Nyarigoti and his colleagues were not aware that Otenyo and his group of warriors were lying in the bush waiting for them. The warriors had decided to attack and punish intruders because of their injustices.

These foreigners did not know that Abagusii had vowed not to rest until they had overpowered the British and secured their land.

In a twinkle of an eye, Otenyo stood from the bush with lightning speed, he raised his spear with his right hand and pulled it back above his shoulder while aiming it at Nyarigoti.

"*Omomura ekebega!* I'm a strong man!" Otenyo uttered as he released the spear that exploded and flew through the air like a bullet.

His aim was on target. The spear 'obeyed its master's will' and pierced Nyarigoti in the chest. Like his fellow officers, he had no idea that they had been targeted. He fell down with a thud. He started bleeding forming a pool of blood where he lay.

Otenyo's heroic act encouraged his colleagues to heighten their attacks against the British officers. They realized that Europeans, like Africans, were not indestructible metals. Like any human beings, they could die from being wounded with spears and arrows.

That attack prompted a brutal, ferocious, and violent confrontation between Otenyo and his warriors on one side and the British officers who fired blindly on the other.

Their guns erupted loudly and violently like thunder. Arrows filled the air producing whistling sounds as they zoomed in search of their targets. This battle was one of a kind that had never been witnessed in this locality before. After firing his spear, Otenyo resorted to fight the enemy with bow and arrows. Soon his arrows ran out. He then decided to engage the enemy in a hand to hand combat.

Pa.... papaaa ... pa ... Darkness! Otenyo's determination was stopped suddenly by the British soldier's bullets. The now angry foreign fighters directed an array of bullets at him. Otenyo got seriously injured and fell hard to the ground, like a banana trunk during a heavy rainstorm. On seeing what had happened to him, his colleagues realized that Moraa's medicine was of no defense against British bullets. They promptly took off.

Shortly afterwards, the British officers arrested Otenyo. Eventually, his blood-soaked torso that was full of bullet wounds was found dumped near a bridge in Kitutu area.

Under the leadership of the Abagusii community, Otenyo's torso was buried on Manga ridge. His head was never found. Otenyo and his fellow heroes who died in their efforts to defend the property, interests and rights of Abagusii are still remembered for their bravery through various songs.

Nyarigoti narrowly escaped death although he was seriously injured from the encounter with Otenyo. This incident sparked intense hostility and confrontations between the British and Abagusii community.

Chinkororo fought the British with inferior weapons such as spears and shields, bows and arrows, slingshots and sticks, while the British used guns.

In that battle, about two hundred young men from the *Chinkororo* defence force were killed. The community was dispossessed of their livestock and their houses were burnt.

After that war, many Britons moved to Kisii town and settled there. This situation caused the town to be called "Bosongo", the European dwelling in the local Ekegusii language.

The British started to undermine the customs and traditions of their hosts by calling them "barbaric".

Because of increased British injustices against Abagusii, there arose a religious sect among them that believed that Sakagwa would return one day and save the people of his community from the repressive British rule. They were inspired in belief by the mysterious manner in which Sakagwa "died".

This belief spread fast like a dry season fire throughout Gusii land. This forced the British to arrest leaders of the sect in order to protect and maintain their interests.

The British wanted to suppress the spread of the belief in the "Shadow of Sakagwa". Those arrested included Kabari, Oguora, Ongeri, Bonareri, Nyakundi, Kemunto, Orioki and Nyamachare.

Sakagwa remains on the lips of the Abagusii people to this day. His last and mysterious words in the Ekegusii language that, "*amandegere name Getembe, ore n'abamura nayae*", mushrooms will bloom in Getembe and only one with sons would harvest them, are still remembered and cherished by Abagusii people.

Stories about Sakagwa will probably continue to be steered in the memory of each generation in his community. His "death" remains a mystifying riddle that will continue to puzzle many in the Abagusii community.

–End-

14. Glossary of Terms

Amarengari:	phantoms or ghosts
Amatimo (sing. *ritimo*):	spears
Amanagu/ rinagu:	black night shade; a popular vegetable among the Abagusii community.
Busaa:	a traditional beer or brew.
Chinduruche:	slingshots
Chinkororo:	young Abagusii men who are specially trained to defend the community against attacks from neighbouring ethnic communities.
Ebitureri (sing. *egetureri*):	trumpets
Enyameni:	wrestling
Erioba:	sun, sky
Engoro:	the name of God in traditional Gusii (Abagusii).
Ekerecha (Pl. *ebirecha*):	spirit.
Emeino(sing. *omoino*):	songs sung by elders when drinking traditional beer.
Ekee (pl. *ebie*):	a kind of bowl made of sorghum straw, strings, and hide skins.
Ensio (pl. *chinsio*):	a small grindstone used to grind grains such as millet into flour.
Mwarobaini:	Neem; type of tree that is used to treat over forty diseases.

Nyomba ya baiseke bange 'nkerandi getakuoma:	a popular Gusii proverb that says that a family with many girls is like a gourd of milk that never runs dry (because the girls' suitors continually pay dowry for them in the form of cows.
Ntomocha:	Let us not be defeated.
Omoragori (pl. *abaragori*):	diviner, a traditional healer.
Omogambi (pl. *abagambi*):	a traditional Gusii chief or leader.
Obokano (pl. *amakano*):	a traditional eight-stringed zither or guitar.
Omoroka:	a short leafy shrub (coleus barbatus) which has soft velvet leaves and a sharp strong smell that is used to make hedges.
Omomura ekebega:	a strong young man.
Orogena (pl. *chingena*):	a big base grindstone that is used with *ensio* (a small upper grindstone) to grind grains especially finger millet into flour.
Ribina:	a traditional Gusii women's dance staged to beseech the gods for rain.

About the Author

Bitugi Matundura was born in Bomoseri, Kisii County. He grew up in Kericho where he attended Kipketer Primary School and later joined the renowned Starehe Boys' Centre & School in Nairobi. He then pursued a Bachelor's degree in Education at Moi University.

After graduation, Matundura joined the Kenya Broadcasting Corporation (KBC) as an editor before enrolling in the University of Nairobi for postgraduate studies in Kiswahili Literature and Linguistics.

He worked briefly for the Nation Media Group as a translator and news writer for Taifa Leo, Daily Nation, and Sunday Nation.

Driven by passion for academia, he left media to focus on education.

Matundura is a renowned literary author, who has written several children's books, many of which have been recommended for use in primary schools by the Kenya Institute of Curriculum Development (KICD).

One of his books, *Sitaki Iwe Siri* [I don't want it to be secret] (by Longhorn Publishers, Nairobi) won a second place in the Jomo Kenyatta Prize for Literature Award in 2009. This is a prestigious literary award in East and Central Africa.

His other works include *Mkasa wa Shujaa Liyongo* [The Tragedy of Hero Liyongo, Phoenix, 2001], *Mwepesi wa Kusahau* [Quick to Forget, Phoenix, 2005], *Masagisa na Zimwi Mbilikimo* [Exploits of the Dwarf Devil, Phoenix, 2007], *Fahali Mtoboa Siri* [Pride of the Secret Revealer, Focus, 2008], *Maadui wa Maria* [Mary's Enemies, Vide – Muwa, 2008], *Jumamosi ya Mkosi* [Tragic Saturday, Phoenix, 2008], *Kisa Cha Nyange* [Nyange's Story, E.A.E.P, 2009], *Mamba Mnafiki* [The Hypocritic Crocodile, E.A.E.P, 2009], and *Mbwa na Sungura* [The Dog and the Rabbit, E.A.E.P, 2009].

He has also published *Masaibu ya Mfalme Tapwara* [The Tribulations of King Tapwara, Jomo Kenyatta Foundation, 2010], *Tatizo la Kisauni* [The problem of Kisauni, Oxford, 2010], *Hazina ya Zuena na Makombo* [The Treasure of Zuena and Makombo, Kenya Literature Bureau, 2010], and *Adhabu ya Joka* [The Dragon's Punishment, Vide-Muwa, 2010].

His collections of short stories include *Mrithi Nini Wanangu?* [What Will You Inherit my Children, KLB], *Shetani Hana Hatia* [The Devil is not Guilty, Focus], **Giza la Kumi Kumi** [The Danger of Cheap Alcohol, Phoenix], *Vyangu Utavilia Kaburini* [Rob Me over My Dead Body, E.A.E.P] and *Karakana ya Mauti* [The Workshop of Death, Longman]. Matundura has also published in academic journals.

This author, a former lecturer at the Catholic University of Eastern Africa (CUEA), currently teaches Kiswahili Literature and literature at Chuka University, where he is also pursuing his doctoral studies in lexicography.

Matundura deliberately writes in Kiswahili because of its prestige and heritage.